Arizona

By Michelle Aki Becker

Consultant
Nanci R. Vargus, Ed.D.
Assistant Professor of Literacy
University of Indianapolis, Indianapolis, Indiana

Children's Press®
A Division of Scholastic Inc.
New York Toronto London Auckland Sydney
Mexico City New Delhi Hong Kong
Danbury, Connecticut

Designer: Herman Adler Design
Photo Researcher: Caroline Anderson
The photo on the cover shows Oregon Pipe Cactus National Park.

Library of Congress Cataloging–in–Publication Data

Becker, Michelle Aki.
  Arizona / by Michelle Aki Becker.
      p. cm. — (Rookie read–about geography)
  Includes index.
  Summary: A simple introduction to Arizona, focusing on its geographical
  features and points of interest.
    ISBN 0-516-22734-3 (lib. bdg.)   0-516-24434-5 (pbk.)
    1. Arizona—Juvenile literature. 2. Arizona—Geography—Juvenile
  literature. [1. Arizona.] I. Title. II. Series.
    F811.3.B43 2004
    917.9'1—dc22

                                        2003016897

CHILDREN'S PRESS, and ROOKIE READ-ABOUT®,
and associated logos are trademarks and or registered trademarks
of Scholastic Library Publishing. SCHOLASTIC and associated logos
are trademarks and or registered trademarks of Scholastic Inc.

1 2 3 4 5 6 7 8 9 10 R 13 12 11 10 09 08 07 06 05 04

Have you ever seen the Grand Canyon?

The Grand Canyon is in Arizona. Can you find Arizona on this map?

It is a state in the southwestern part of the United States.

CANADA

WASHINGTON

OREGON

IDAHO

MONTANA

NORTH DAKOTA

SOUTH DAKOTA

WYOMING

MINNESOTA

WISCONSIN

MICHIGAN

NEW HAMPSHIRE

VERMONT

MAINE

NEVADA

UTAH

COLORADO

NEBRASKA

IOWA

NEW YORK

MASSACHUSETTS

RHODE ISLAND

CONNECTICUT

NEW JERSEY

CALIFORNIA

ARIZONA

NEW MEXICO

KANSAS

ILLINOIS

INDIANA

OHIO

PENNSYLVANIA

WEST VIRGINIA

DELAWARE

MARYLAND

Washington, D.C.

MISSOURI

KENTUCKY

VIRGINIA

OKLAHOMA

ARKANSAS

TENNESSEE

NORTH CAROLINA

TEXAS

LOUISIANA

MISSISSIPPI

ALABAMA

GEORGIA

SOUTH CAROLINA

FLORIDA

ALASKA

CANADA

MEXICO

HAWAII

North

West

East

South

5

6

Some of Arizona is
a desert (DEH-zert).

A desert is a hot, dry
place. Cactus plants
grow in the desert.

Rattlesnakes, prairie dogs, and other animals live in the desert.

Gila Monster

The cactus wren is the state bird.

The Colorado River runs
through Arizona.

Water from the river
has carved out the Grand
Canyon. It has worn away
the rock over many years.

There are fossils (FAH-sels)
in the Grand Canyon. They
are hidden in the rocks.

Fossils are remains of
plants and animals that
lived long ago.

More than 4 million people visit the Grand Canyon each year.

They learn about the canyon from park rangers.

A long time ago, the Anasazi (ah-nah-SAH-zee) built homes in the cliffs.

The Anasazi were Native Americans.

People in Arizona don't live in the cliffs anymore. They live in all kinds of homes.

The biggest city in Arizona is Phoenix (FEE-niks). It is also the state capital.

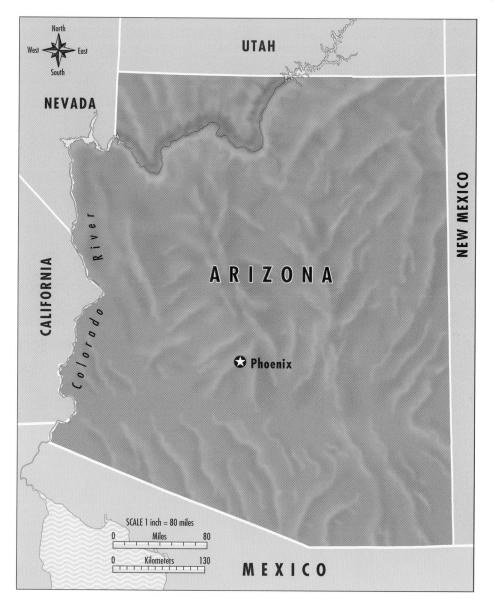

21

Many people in Arizona work in factories. They make computers and airplane parts.

Others are farmers who grow cotton, lettuce, and other crops. There are also miners who dig for copper.

Lettuce

People of all ages like to
visit or live in Arizona.

They like the warm weather
and the natural wonders.

What do you like best
about Arizona?

Words You Know

Anasazi home

cactus

cactus wren

desert

30

fossil

Grand Canyon

lettuce

Phoenix

31

Index

About the Author

Michelle Aki Becker often travels around the country and writes geography books for children. She enjoys learning about the history of a state and visiting its landmarks.

Photo Credits

Photographs © 2004: Bob & Suzanne Clemenz: cover, 10, 14, 25, 26, 27, 29; Corbis Images/John Maher: 22; Dembinsky Photo Assoc.: 9, 30 bottom left (Jim Battles), 13 (Dominique Braud), 6, 30 bottom right, 30 top right (Willard Clay); Peter Arnold Inc.: 8 (John Cancalosi), 3, 31 top right (John Kieffer); Robertstock.com/G.L. French: 18; Tom Bean: 12, 31 top left; Tom Till Photography, Inc.: 17, 30 top left.

Maps by Bob Italiano.